Look and Find

**Cover illustrated by
Arkadia Illustration and Design Limited**

Endsheets illustrated by Amy Shutz

Illustrated by Animagination, Inc.

Written by Lee Cooper, Elle Hikkum,
Nancy L. McGill, Trudy Nickels, and Dakota Wolf

Lettered by Walter Wilson

Published by
Louis Weber, C.E.O.
Publications International, Ltd.
7373 North Cicero Avenue
Lincolnwood, Illinois 60646

READING

© 1996 Warner Bros.

Manufactured in U.S.A.

8 7 6 5 4 3 2 1

ISBN 0-7853-1873-9

PUBLICATIONS INTERNATIONAL, LTD.

It's a slow day at Moron Mountain. Swackhammer, the head honcho of this failing intergalactic theme park, is looking for fun in all the wrong places. He's got to find something to spice up his act, and it looks like planet Earth is just what the "doc" ordered! If only he had some Looney Tunes at his theme park—then he would be the biggest star in space!

Keep an eye out for these Nerdlucks, Swackhammer's alien assistants. They're loonier than they look!

Bang

Pound

Bupkus

Zippo

Blanko

Neinte

Nil

The aliens have landed! The aliens have landed! Swackhammer's swanky alien crew has set down in Looney Tune Land, and these Nerdlucks aren't leaving until the Looney Tunes agree to entertain the extraterrestrials for eons. A bit of a bargain is what the Looney Tunes need to keep from being slaves among the stars.

Look for these panicked Looney Tunes as they rush to help Bugs Bunny fight for their freedom.

Elmer Fudd

Michigan J. Frog

Daffy Duck

Foghorn Leghorn

Road Runner

Sylvester and Sylvester Jr.

Granny

It's game night at Madison Square Garden, and the crowd is going wild! But a few unexpected fans sent by Swackhammer are here to steal some NBA players' pizazz and make an all-star team of their own! The Looney Tunes have challenged the Nerdlucks to a basketball game to battle for their freedom not knowing that those puny little Nerdlucks had a nasty plan to win the game.

While the Nerdlucks scope out the best basketball players, find these silly vendors in the crowd.

Candy

Frank

Curly

Red

Slim

Pops

After their first practice is a flop, the Looney Tunes have no choice but to go pro. Michael Jordan had an easy afternoon of golf in mind, but the Looney Tunes have another idea. It looks like Michael's golfing days are over: He's being drafted by the Tune Squad for the biggest game of his life.

Look around the golf course for these golf-related goodies.

This golf ball

A birdie

Stan

A Bogey

This seven iron

Caddy Jack

Joe Pro

A hole in one

Emergency! The Looney Tunes' lives are in danger if they don't get Michael Jordan on their team! They need his sensational basketball skills to overcome the Nerdlucks, who, with the essence of some of the greatest NBA players, have become the Monstars! Convincing Michael to play for the Tune Squad is going to take the skill of a surgeon. Watch as Ductor Daffy makes Michael Jordan open up and say, "Ahhh!"

As the Looney Tunes persuade Michael to join their team, find these crazy characters.

Candy Striper

Chief Resident

Ductor Quack

Harry Healer

Witch Doctor

Florence Nightgown

CHICAGO

ALL STARS

With Michael finally on their team, detective Daffy and bungling Bugs are on a mission to find his basketball gear. Between the mess of Michael's trophy room and the menace of his bulldog, Charles, Bugs and Daffy may never make it to the big game alive!

Can you find Bugs and Michael's things in all this pandemonium?

These shoes

Bungling Bugs

45 jersey

Beanie the bull

Gold medal

Charles

This championship trophy

1993

Aaaand now! The Tune Squad takes the court to battle the Monstars in the Ultimate Game. It looks as if the Looney Tunes are taking a beating—literally! Michael Jordan is the only one who can dodge the blows of the Monstars and make it to the basket to score. Michael seems to be everywhere at once.

Look around the court to find the Looney Tunes—or what is left of them, anyway.

Tweety

Porky Pig

Bugs Bunny

Lola Bunny

Daffy Duck

Marvin the Martian

Yosemite Sam

It is Monstars 64 to Tune Squad 18 at the half, and the battered Looneys have lost their tune. As the dejected team gathers to moan about its pains and listens to Michael's pep talk, Bugs whips up a secret solution to boost team spirit.

Can you find these locker room items among the tired Looney Tunes?

A Tunes towel

A Jordan jersey

Wacky weights

Smelly socks

Spacey swimsuit

Baseball bat

A Looney lunch box

Michael sinks the shot of the century in the last seconds and leads the Tune Squad to victory! The aliens are so impressed with the Tunes' team spirit that they decide to become part of the gang. Looks like everyone's a winner here except Swackhammer, who has just "high-tailed" it back to Moron Mountain.

Keep an eye out for all these signs of a big win.

Checkered flag

A blowout

Final score

Bull's-eye

Victory kiss

Blanket of roses

Gold medal

TUNES WIN!

MON ARS

TUNES

It doesn't get any stupider than Moron Mountain! Go back for another ride and find these moronic things.

Dodo bird
Crash dummy
Dumb jock
Dumbbell
Dumb waiter
Dumbstruck

The Nerdlucks aren't the only alien articles in Looney Tune Land. Go back and find these items that are out of this world.

Dog star
Green card
Milky Way
Black hole
Comet
Flying cup and saucer
Big Dipper

Hey, sports fans, there's still time on the clock! Go back to Madison Square Garden to find these other "fans."

"Fan"ny pack
Fan letter
Polka-dotted fan
"Fan"tom
A "fan"g
A "fan"cy dress

A lot more than the occasional ball gets lost on a golf course! Go back to the golf course where Michael gets abducted by Looney Tunes and find these other out-of-place items.

Spare tire
Persian Golf
Monkey wrench
Golf of Mexico
Baseball bat
Golf tea
The kitchen sink